Great Adventurers

Great Adventurers

David Walter

First published in 1978 by
Macdonald Educational Ltd
Holywell House
Worship Street
London EC2A 2EN

© Macdonald Educational 1978

ISBN 0-382-06295-7
Published in the
United States by
Silver Burdett
Company, Morristown, N.J.
1979 Printing
Library of Congress
Catalog Card No. 79-64163

Contents

Odysseus: the taste for adventure

▼ It was thanks to Odysseus' cunning that the Greeks captured Troy. He and his men built a wooden horse and hid inside it. The Trojans thought the horse had a magic power to protect them and they dragged it into the city. The Greeks sprang out In the night and took the city.

Odysseus, the hero of Greek myth, was the original great adventurer. In fact, the title of the story of his travels, the *Odyssey*, has become a word for an adventurous journey. He had enormous powers of endurance. He was cunning. He could turn his hand to anything. The mythical hero had all the qualities which real-life pioneers have shown down the centuries.

The *Odyssey* is the story of Odysseus' ten year journey back from the Trojan War to his home. We discover him first on the island of Ogygia, where he has been held captive by the goddess Calypso for seven years. The gods order Calypso to release him, so she allows him to build a boat on which to escape.

When Odysseus has been sailing for 17 days, his enemy Poseidon, the god of the sea, causes a tremendous storm. Odysseus is shipwrecked. He has to swim for two days and nights before reaching land.

He lands in a friendly country, and his hosts ask him to tell them about his adventures. Among stories he relates is the following one about his escape from the one-eyed giant Polyphemus.

Odysseus and his companions reached the island where Polyphemus lived and started exploring an enormous cave. Suddenly the owner came home. His appearance terrified them. They were even more scared when he ate two of them for his supper.

It was no use killing him while he was asleep because he had rolled an enormous boulder over the entrance to the cave. It was far too heavy for the Greeks to lift. Then Odysseus had a brainwave. He gave Polyphemus some very good wine he had brought with him. When the giant fell into a drunken stupor, Odysseus and four other men took an enormous staff which they found in the cave. They heated the staff on the fire and thrust it into his eye.

▼ Odysseus to the rescue again. The goddess Circe turned half of his crew into pigs. With a drug to counteract her spells, Odysseus got the better of Circe and had his men restored to human form.

▶ On the way back from Troy, Odysseus visited the land of the Lotus-Eaters. Some of his men ate the lotus fruit, which made them want to forget their homes and stay there. Odysseus had to drag them away.

▲ A Greek vase painting of Odysseus blinding Polyphemus.

In the morning, Polyphemus, blind and mad with pain, rolled away the boulder to let his sheep out. He stood at the entrance of the cave, stretching his hands out to make sure that the Greeks did not escape. However, Odysseus and his men tied themselves underneath the sheep and made their getaway.

Odysseus had many other adventures, some of which are illustrated on this page. Eventually his ship was wrecked. All his crew were drowned, and he alone escaped to Calypso's island.

The legend of Odysseus has captured the imagination of people through the ages. Its theme of a man stretched to the limits of his resources finds an echo in the exploits of the men and women described in the following pages.

▼ All who heard the Sirens sing wanted to stay and listen for ever. When his ship sailed past them, Odysseus put wax in his men's ears so that they could not hear the magical music. He had himself lashed to the mast, so that he could hear, but had to sail on.

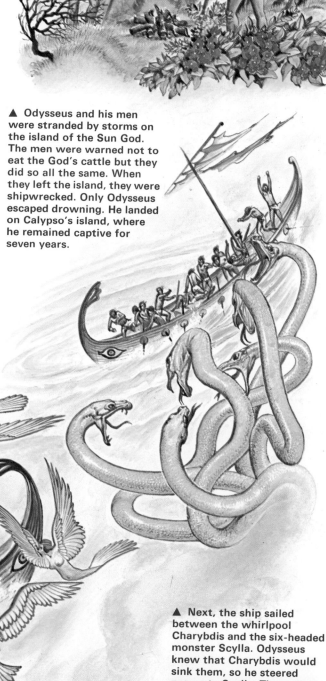

▲ Odysseus and his men were stranded by storms on the island of the Sun God. The men were warned not to eat the God's cattle but they did so all the same. When they left the island, they were shipwrecked. Only Odysseus escaped drowning. He landed on Calypso's island, where he remained captive for seven years.

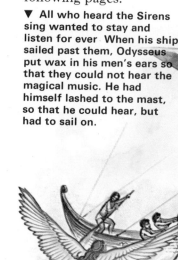

▲ Next, the ship sailed between the whirlpool Charybdis and the six-headed monster Scylla. Odysseus knew that Charybdis would sink them, so he steered nearer to Scylla. The monster grabbed six men as the ship passed but the rest of the crew were safe.

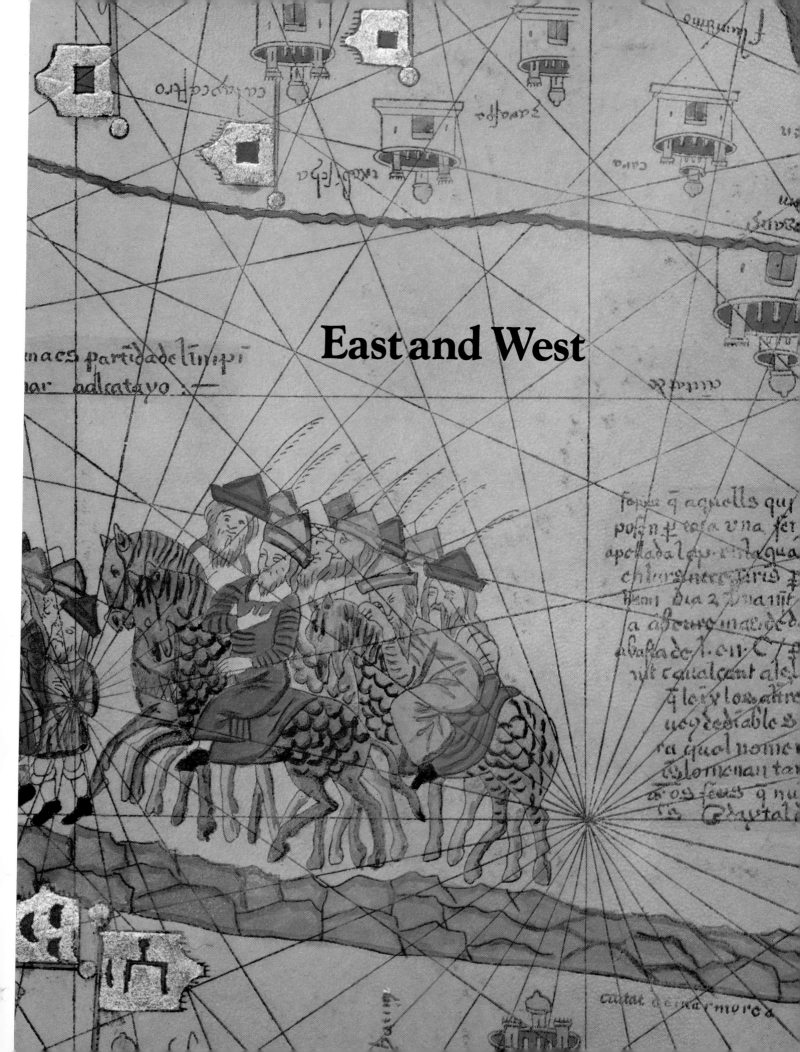

East and West

Friar Carpini: a journey into Mongolia

The journey from Lyon in France to Karakoram in Mongolia takes you nearly half way round the world. The round trip would be daunting in the 20th century, let alone the 13th. It was astonishing that a fat friar, more than 60 years old, could go there and back at that time and survive to tell the tale.

Friar Giovanni de Piano Carpini's mission was to deliver a letter from the Pope to the Great Khan of the Mongols. It must have been the longest postman's round in history. Carpini was sent because of the widespread fear that Ogedai, the Great Khan, planned an attack on Western Europe.

Luckily for Europe, Ogedai died. The Mongol army, under the leadership of General Batu, had to return to the capital for the election of a new Great Khan. It was at this point that Pope Innocent IV sent Carpini off with a letter asking the Mongols to 'give over their bloody slaughter of mankind and to receive the Christian faith'.

Carpini was accompanied by another friar, Benedict of Poland, and five servants. The journey was reasonable until they got to Kiev, where they saw the sort of destruction of which the Mongols were capable. Kiev had been the finest city in Russia. Batu's army had reduced it to 200 houses. Carpini was horrified by the number of dead men's bones he found around the city.

The friars pressed on. They followed the method the Mongols had devised for fast travel across the Steppes. Every few kilometres, they changed ponies so as to cover as great a distance as possible during a day. The tired riders often travelled far into the night and went whole days without a meal.

At last they reached Syra Ordu, the summer court of the Great Khan near Karakoram. They had travelled 4,800 kilometres in just over 100 days. They spent four months at Syra Ordu. During this time Carpini learnt a great deal about the Mongol Empire.

Kuyuk, the newly elected Khan, did not take Carpini's presence seriously. He treated the Pope's letter as an offer of submission, and sent instructions to him to come in person and pay homage.

Carpini's journey back was gruelling. It was winter and he and his companions often had to make a primitive camp in the snow. At Kiev, they were greeted as if they had returned from the dead. They finally reached Lyon over two years after they had first set out.

The information Carpini brought back was never put to use, as the threatened invasion did not materialize. But the incredible expedition of the fat friar opened the eyes of people in the West to a new world.

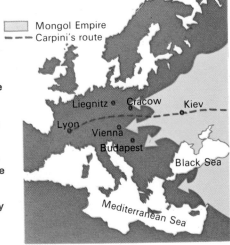

▶ At the time of Carpini's journey, the Mongol Empire stretched from China to Eastern Europe. Genghis Khan, the founder of the dynasty, had unified the many Mongol tribes into one nation, and gone on to conquer much of China and Russia. Under Genghis's son Ogedai, the general Batu swept through the rest of Russia, destroyed the Polish city of Cracow and overcame Hungary. Most of Carpini's route to the court of the Great Khan at Karakoram lay through lands which had recently been laid waste by the Mongols.

☐ Mongol Empire
- - - Carpini's route

Liegnitz • Cracow • Kiev
Lyon
Vienna
Budapest
Black Sea
Mediterranean Sea

▲ Friar Giovanni de Piano Carpini, the first European to cross Asia. He was over 60 years old when he made his journey, and extremely fat.

▶ Before Carpini, Westerners regarded the Mongols as bloodthirsty savages. In fact, their tactics in battle were very elaborate. Their cavalry was the fastest in the world.

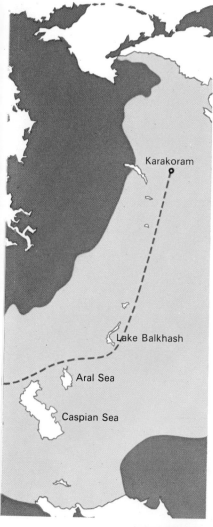

▲ The Steppes stretch over 2,250,000 kilometres of what is now the Soviet Union. The terrain is dry grassland, with few trees. In winter, the temperature can be as low as −30°C (−22°F). Carpini found the journey gruelling.

► Kuyuk Khan, grandson of Genghis. The highlight of Carpini's stay in Mongolia was Kuyuk's coronation, which was attended by 3,000 ambassadors and princes from all over the Mongol Empire.

▼ The Mongols were nomads. They had a type of tent called a yurt, which could be carried on the backs of two camels and put up in half an hour. The framework was stretched out, covered with tightly woven felt and bound together with ropes. A carpet served as a door.

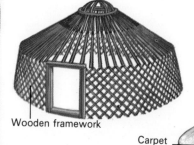

Wooden framework

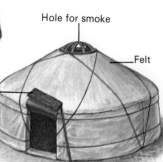

Hole for smoke

Felt

Carpet

Cheng Ho: from East to West

Westerners often imagine that the history of exploration and discovery through the ages belongs to them alone. People in other countries, they think, spent all those centuries just sitting there waiting to be discovered by somebody like Carpini. In fact, the Hindus, the Arabs and the Chinese can all boast of travellers of the distant past whose feats rival anything attempted by their contemporaries in Europe.

A generation before the birth of Christopher Columbus, the Chinese admiral Cheng Ho set off on the first of seven epic voyages. The new Ming emperor had chosen the title Yung-lo, meaning 'eternal contentment', for his reign, but he was certainly restless to discover new lands. He sent Cheng Ho out with a huge fleet to impress foreign countries with the wealth and power of China, and persuade them to accept Chinese sovereignty. He was also to bring back new luxuries for the imperial court.

Cheng Ho's expeditions led 30 countries to bear tribute to the emperor. Among other places, his fleets sailed to Java, Sumatra, India, Aden and East Africa. Enormous distances were involved, for which the expeditions were well equipped. The fleet consisted of 60 vast treasure-ships, each carrying 500 men.

Cheng Ho's own account of his travels was unfortunately destroyed. However, there are other works which survive to provide a flavour of the voyages. The interpreter Ma Huan wrote about the Nicobar Islands in the Bay of Bengal. He describes how the people went about naked. They had a legend, he says, that if they were to put on even the scantiest articles of clothing, they would break out in sores. This was because Buddha had put a curse on their ancestors for stealing his clothes while he was bathing.

▼ Chinese junks were broad and almost square. They could carry up to 700 men.

▼ Making porcelain became big business during the Ming period. Cheng Ho's ships would have probably carried vases like this for export.

▲ During the reign of Emperor Yung-lo, the Ming dynasty was at its height. After his death naval expeditions came to an end.

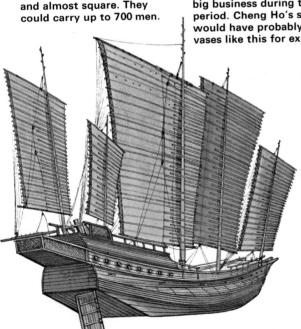

Ma Huan also went to Ceylon (Sri Lanka). He climbed a high mountain near the King's residence. There he saw something which was said to be a footprint, 3 metres in length. It was supposed to have been made by the first man. Ma Huan calls him A-Tan, but it is the same man as the Adam of the Bible.

Another of Cheng Ho's crew, Fei Hsin, has an account of Djube in East Africa. 'The products of the country', he writes, 'are lions, gold-spotted leopards and camel-birds, which are six or seven feet tall'. These camel-birds must have been ostriches.

The Chinese court had a great fascination for exotic animals. On one expedition Cheng Ho's job was to escort home ambassadors from Melinda in East Africa. These ambassadors had heard of Cheng Ho's expeditions and China's power, and had brought a giraffe to the emperor as a tribute gift. The Chinese took the giraffe to be a unicorn, a magical beast in their tradition. Apart from the physical resemblance, the word the ambassadors used for giraffe, *girin*, sounded like the Chinese word for unicorn, *ch'i-lin*.

The power of the Ming dynasty declined under the next emperor and the voyages came to an end. Cheng Ho had brought the Chinese into contact with numerous peoples of whom they had had little or no knowledge before. If the emperor had not stopped his expeditions, he might have beaten Columbus across the Atlantic.

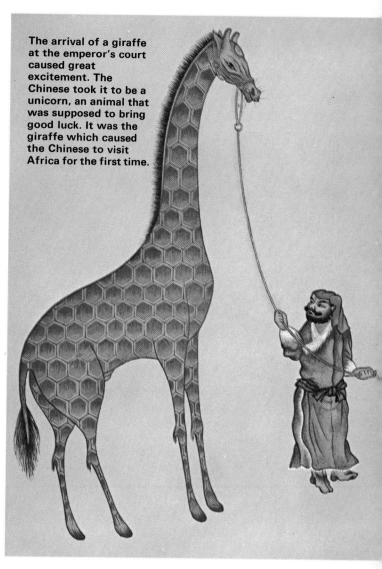

The arrival of a giraffe at the emperor's court caused great excitement. The Chinese took it to be a unicorn, an animal that was supposed to bring good luck. It was the giraffe which caused the Chinese to visit Africa for the first time.

▼ A copy of part of a map of Cheng Ho's travels. Unlike European maps of the same period, it is a true mariner's chart with compass bearings. It is not drawn to scale, however. The dotted lines at the top of the map indicate Cheng Ho's route along the east coast of India, those towards the bottom his route along the east coast of Africa.

The Chinese Compass

The Chinese used compasses long before the Europeans or the Arabs. The earliest type consisted of a wooden spoon, representing the constellation of the Great Bear. A small magnet was fitted to the end of the bowl, so that when it was balanced, the handle pointed south. The later example shown above consists of a magnetized iron needle placed in straw floating in water.

Walter Ralegh: the search for El Dorado

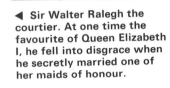

◀ Sir Walter Ralegh the courtier. At one time the favourite of Queen Elizabeth I, he fell into disgrace when he secretly married one of her maids of honour.

▲ *Indians dancing*, a drawing by John White, the Governor of the colony which Ralegh founded in America. Many colonists treated the Indians badly.

'I will undertake there was never any prison in England that could be found more unsavoury and loathsome...' Walter Ralegh had reached the River Orinoco, and he did not much like what he found there.

Since 1584, Ralegh had been sending expeditions across the Atlantic to his colony in Virginia, the first British settlement on American soil. Now, ten years later, his fortune had changed. He was in disgrace at Court. In an attempt to restore himself to favour with Queen Elizabeth I, he decided to cross the ocean himself in a wild adventure.

Ralegh had heard a story about a land called El Dorado, where there were fabulous quantities of gold. The King of El Dorado was supposed to have a garden where he kept life-size copies in precious metal of everything which lived or grew in his country. People believed El Dorado lay in the Highlands of Guiana, and that was where Ralegh's expedition was heading.

Ralegh had a hundred men with him. His route to the Highlands lay through the wide delta of the Orinoco River inland, and the water was too shallow for anything except for open boats. Soon the party was lost in the maze of streams running through the delta. They managed to capture an old Indian to guide them, but after rowing for four days, they were almost out of food and drink, and they had seen nothing.

In the nick of time, they found a village. Ralegh ordered his men not to harm or steal from the Indians. The local chief Toparacima lent him another guide to help the expedition on its way.

Ralegh's main objective was, of course, gold. However he also had to satisfy his curiosity about a great many other things which he found on the way. He had a fascination for medicine. When he met some Indians who used poisoned arrows, he questioned them at length about the poison and the remedy for it.

Ralegh's medical advice to his party seems to have been successful. Despite the climate and the insects, none of his companions caught any fatal diseases. Years later, when he was a prisoner in the Tower of London, Ralegh produced a 'balsam of Guiana.' This so impressed Queen Anne that she was in favour of releasing Ralegh against the wishes of her husband King James, who had succeeded Elizabeth to the throne.

At last the expedition came in sight of the Highlands, where El Dorado was supposed to lie. Here, Ralegh's party found rocks which looked as if they contained gold and silver. Ralegh returned home with these rocks, which he believed would be proof that there was indeed fabulous wealth in Guiana. The rocks turned out to be worthless. Ralegh's pride was wounded still further when people scoffed at his stories. They claimed that he had been skulking in Cornwall all the time and had never set foot in South America at all.

Ralegh continued to believe in El Dorado. Twenty years later, King James released him from the Tower for a second journey to Guiana. It was this ill-fated voyage which led to his trial and execution.

Ralegh was much more than a crude swashbuckler. He may have failed to find El Dorado, but he set high standards of behaviour towards the Indians on his expedition. He also made observations which advanced geography, science and natural history. Ralegh, the sea captain, the colonist, the popularizer of tobacco, the courtier and the historian may have overshadowed Ralegh the explorer, but his journey up the Orinoco would have been a sufficient achievement on its own for anybody else.

▲ Ralegh was taken in by Indian stories of the Ewaipanoma, the men whose heads grew beneath their shoulders.

▶ It was seeing such extraordinary sights as the armadillo (right) that made him ready to believe almost anything.

Haute. Armadillo.

▲ Finding the way through the winding tributaries of the Orinoco River was not an easy task for Ralegh and his men. The dense vegetation reaching down to the water's edge made every stream look the same.

The Myth of El Dorado

It is not surprising that so many Elizabethans came to believe in the myth of El Dorado. Two generations before Ralegh, the Spaniard Francisco Pizarro had

discovered and conquered the Inca Empire of Peru. There he had found a highly developed civilization, which produced fabulous golden treasures, like this ceremonial knife (left). Further north, the Spaniards had found equally spectacular wealth in Mexico such as the gold mask (right).

The main evidence for the existence of El Dorado came from the story told by one of Pizarro's men. He claimed he had been set adrift in a canoe as a punishment, and had floated in it down to Manoa, the capital of El Dorado. There he said he had seen huge quantities of gold, and that he had been present at a ceremony where dozens of chief citizens had covered their bodies in powdered gold.

Richard Burton: journey to Mecca

It was rather a squash on the ship to say the least. The *Golden Wire* was built to hold 60 passengers, but there were 97 Moslem pilgrims aboard on their way across the Red Sea to the holy cities of Mecca and Medina. It was not surprising that a riot broke out. Daggers were drawn and men were injured. Eventually, a 'Moslem doctor from India' who was on the upper deck poured an enormous jar of water onto the rioters below, and the trouble died down.

None of the pilgrims on board guessed that the man who had drenched them was not an Indian or a Moslem at all. He was an Englishman in disguise, and his name was Richard Burton. Burton was to become one of the great explorers of Africa. Unlike most of his contemporaries, his fascination for exotic places was equalled by a fascination for their people. He did not share the feelings of superiority which other Victorian Englishmen had towards non-Europeans. Instead he tried to live as they did and learn to understand them.

Mecca and Medina are the holy cities of Mohammedanism. They are forbidden to those who do not share the faith. Two non-believers had been discovered and executed only eight years before Burton's visit. The official penalty had been relaxed in the meantime, but, if he had been caught, Burton could have expected outraged pilgrims to take the law into their own hands and slit his throat.

One or two other Europeans had managed to penetrate Mecca, but none had returned with a really thorough description of the city. Burton wanted to make accurate measurements and to take notes, but this was not easy. He carried a sextant at the start of his journey, but his Arab servant was so suspicious of it that he had to abandon it.

▲ Richard Burton, explorer, author and linguist. In his lifetime, Burton mastered 29 languages.

▲ Burton disguised himself by staining his face with walnut juice, growing a long beard, shaving his head and wearing Arab dress.

Burton's pilgrimage

Burton set off on his pilgrimage in 1853. First he spent a month in Alexandria, perfecting his knowledge of Arab customs. He went on to Cairo, where he bought supplies and his pilgrim's dress, then by camel to Suez, where he boarded the *Golden Wire*. He landed at Yenbo, and went on again by camel. The pilgrims had to travel much of the way by night.

Alexandria
Cairo
Suez
Akaba
Africa
El Muwaila
ARABIA
Wejh
RED SEA
Medina
Yenbo
Mecca

The Great Mosque at Mecca

The Kaaba
(covered with black silk
with Koran inscriptions)

The Black Stone is
embedded in the S.E.
corner

Zem Zem or the Holy Well
where pilgrims take water

Pilgrims walk anti-clockwise seven
times round the Kaaba, then kiss the
Black Stone

▲ In the Kaaba, Burton performed all the proper rituals. He drank from the holy well, and filled some bottles to take home. He spent a long time kissing and touching the Black Stone, so that he could take a good look at it. He decided it was a meteorite.

◀ Mohammedanism has been the inspiration of many fine works of art. This illustration taken from a Persian manuscript shows holy men and an angel visiting Mohammed.

▼ Before entering the mosque at Mecca, Moslem pilgrims put on these special cotton robes, called the *Ihram*. The men must endure the heat bare-headed. The women have to wear veils.

While wading ashore from the ship at one of its ports of call, Burton stepped on a sea-urchin. His foot became poisoned, and he could only walk with great difficulty. However, he was determined to go on. When the ship reached Yenbo, he continued his journey in a litter strapped to a camel.

He was ambushed on the way to Medina, but survived to make a tour of the shrines there. Then he carried on to Mecca on an inland route which no European had travelled before. He had to escape another ambush before arriving in the sacred city.

The climax of his visit was his entry into the Kaaba, the holy of holies inside the Great Mosque of Mecca. There, he was asked searching questions about his identity, but he was not found out. While he was saying the ritual prayers, Burton managed to draw a sketch-plan.

Burton became friendly with fellow-pilgrims of all classes on his journey. The insights which he gained into Arab life added a great deal to European understanding of the Arab world.

Mary Kingsley

The Victorians called West Africa the 'White Man's Grave'. The idea of a white woman going there alone was absurd. Any woman who attempted it, they thought, might as well be signing her own death warrant.

It was not surprising that when Mary announced her intention of travelling alone to the West African coast, her friends tried to persuade her not to go. The climate was terrible. There were any number of tropical diseases which a European was bound to catch. If that did not put her off, there was the prospect of ending up in a cooking pot, for there were cannibals in the area.

Mary Kingsley went all the same. For years she had been a devoted daughter, helping her father, looking after her invalid mother, hardly leaving the house. Now, both her parents had died, and it was her chance to explore the world. She wanted to go to West Africa.

She made a preliminary trip, visiting ports along the coast and travelling inland from Luanda in Angola. Then, two years later, she set out on the great adventure of her life, in the cannibal country of Gabon.

The route which Mary planned took her through territory which no European had explored before. At first, she travelled by canoe, in the company of four African tribesmen from the coast. Down the river, she would stop from time to time to trade with villagers.

Soon, Mary was in the unknown territory where the cannibals lived. The tribesmen at the first village seemed hostile, but luckily Kiva, one of the villagers, recognized one of her African guides. The people accepted her, and gave her new guides to take her on foot into the forest.

Her trip was not without incident. On one occasion Mary slipped off a hillside and fell through the roof of a native hut below. For the natives it must have been a startling introduction to the first white person they had ever seen!

Mary gained the respect of her cannibal guides by eating a snake with them, a meal which the Africans from the coast would not touch. On the way to Efoua, the next village, she fell into an elephant trap, but luckily her heavy Victorian skirt stopped her fall, and she was not hurt. In Efoua, she stayed in the chief's hut, surrounded by the decaying remains of the people he had eaten.

The next village, Egaja, had a terrible reputation. Mary managed to survive by producing ointments and medicines for the natives. Her prestige was sufficient to save Kiva from being eaten after he had quarrelled with one of the villagers.

Soon, Mary was back in a village where Europeans were not strangers. Her short journey was an extraordinary feat for a woman in the 19th century. She had been able to overcome the prejudices of her contemporaries and develop an understanding of Africa which put her 50 years ahead of her time.

▲ Mary Kingsley had to wait until she was 30 for the chance to travel. She never married, but found that the Africans accepted her more easily if she said she was searching for her lost husband.

▶ Mary and native porters trudging through the tangled undergrowth of the jungle swamps. The secret of Mary's survival was the trust which she gained from the Africans. Unlike the missionaries of her day, she did not regard them as inferiors, or feel that they needed to be educated out of their ignorance. She respected their traditions and wanted them preserved.

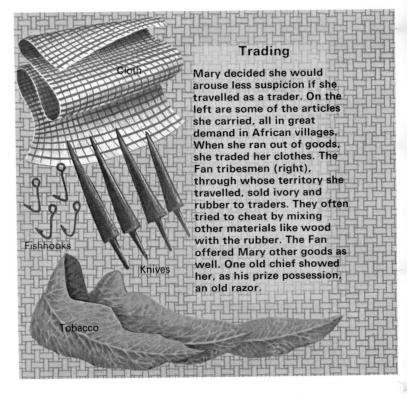

Cloth

Fishhooks

Knives

Tobacco

Trading

Mary decided she would arouse less suspicion if she travelled as a trader. On the left are some of the articles she carried, all in great demand in African villages. When she ran out of goods, she traded her clothes. The Fan tribesmen (right), through whose territory she travelled, sold ivory and rubber to traders. They often tried to cheat by mixing other materials like wood with the rubber. The Fan offered Mary other goods as well. One old chief showed her, as his prize possession, an old razor.

Rubber

Ivory

▼ The original purpose of Mary's journey was to collect rare fish. Despite all her hardships, she was able to find many specimens, not only of fish, but of shells, insects, plants and reptiles. She labelled everything with great care. Several new species of fish which she found were named after her.

Ctenopoma Kingsleyae

Barilius Bibie

Lawrence of Arabia: the call of the desert

As a student, T. E. Lawrence set himself great feats of endurance. He would go swimming on ice-cold winter nights, or bicycle until he collapsed with exhaustion. He worked just as fanatically at his studies, sometimes reading right through the night if a subject engrossed him.

Lawrence had an exceptional store of energy and determination. Soon he found a cause to which he could devote his energies. He had taken a job helping to excavate the ancient city of Carchemish in Syria. While he was there, he became fascinated by the Arab world. He learned Arabic and studied Arab customs. He began too to share the people's dislike of their Turkish rulers, and to dream with them of the day when they could win their freedom.

When World War I broke out, there was a chance that Lawrence's dream might come true. Turkey had sided with Germany against Britain. So it was in the interests of the British to help the Arabs to rebel against the Turks.

Lawrence was posted to British intelligence in Cairo. In 1916, the Arabs revolted, as he had hoped they would. The rebellion, in the area known as the Hejaz, was led by the ruler of Mecca, Sherif Hussein, and his sons Ali, Feisal, Zeid and Abdulla.

The attack on Akaba

Lawrence and the Arabs set out on their long trek across the desert. They carried guns, half a bag of flour each, and £20,000 in gold divided between them as wages for the Howeitat with whom they were to link up.

They had to put up with scorching sandstorms crossing the desert. The storms cracked their lips and chapped their faces. Lawrence's throat became dry and very sore.

Lawrence turns back to find a man who is missing. By the law of the desert, the leader is responsible for his followers. After an hour and a half, Lawrence found the man, who was babbling hysterically through exposure to the sun.

◄ A portrait of Lawrence. It was Feisal who first advised him to wear Arab dress. Lawrence found it more comfortable in the heat than European clothes.

As a decoy movement to confuse the Turks, Lawrence went with a small force to attack the railway near Deraa. They blew up some track, set fire to a station, and, as a bonus, captured a flock of sheep.

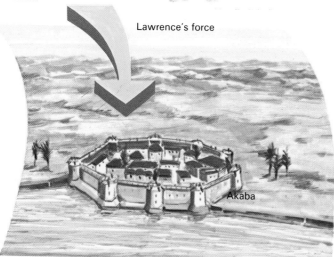

During a battle with Turks Lawrence shot the camel he was riding by mistake and it fell dead beneath him. He narrowly avoided being trampled to death.

Lawrence's force

Akaba

▲ The Turks at Akaba had been expecting an attack from the sea. When Lawrence arrived from inland with the large force he had gathered on his march across the desert, they were forced to surrender.

▶ Lawrence died in a motorcycle accident in 1935. His life after the war had been one of disappointment. To escape the publicity he hated, he had joined the RAF under an assumed name, J. M. Ross.

More conventional army officers found Lawrence conceited and eccentric. However, he managed to obtain leave from his department to take part in talks between the British and Hussein's son Abdulla. Abdulla took to Lawrence and gave him an introduction to his more powerful brother Feisal, who had 8,000 men under arms. Lawrence found him an impressive man, with his long white robes and the scarlet and gold cord around his headdress.

From his meeting with Feisal onwards, Lawrence played a decisive role in the Arab revolt. He persuaded the authorities that the Arabs would not fight alongside British and French troops. Instead, Lawrence went alone to help Feisal in his campaign against the enemy Turks.

Lawrence's sympathy for their way of life meant that he commanded great respect amongst the Arabs. As a result, he was able to co-ordinate the efforts of small, undisciplined tribal armies against the enemy.

One of the most effective forms of damage the Arabs could inflict on the Turks was to dynamite the railway which ran down into the Hejaz from Amman. Lawrence organized many raids on the line, blowing up trains and track.

Before long, the rebels gained control of most of the towns in the area. The big objectives were first Akaba, at the head of the Red Sea, and then Damascus, the capital of Syria. Lawrence's scheme to capture Akaba involved a dangerous 300 kilometre march through the desert to join up with the Howeitat tribesmen to the east of the town.

By the time the Arabs captured Akaba, Lawrence, or al-Urenz as they called him, had become a legend in the desert. He was taken prisoner by the Turks, but escaped. They put up posters offering £20,000 for him alive and £10,000 dead. He surrounded himself with a bodyguard and survived to help the Arabs capture their final goal of Damascus. When they rode into the city, he was greeted as a conquering hero.

Gladys Aylward: to China for God

The transformation of Gladys Aylward, the Cockney parlourmaid, into Ai-weh-deh, Chinese missionary, spy and foot inspector, is one of the most extraordinary stories of the 20th century.

Just after World War I, Gladys was in domestic service in central London. She formed the idea that God had called her to be a missionary in China. Nothing could put her off. She spent a term training with a missionary society, only to be told that she was not clever enough at theology or the Chinese language to be sent to China.

So instead Gladys decided to save up the money to pay for her own journey. She found out that the cheapest way was by rail through Siberia. She worked as much overtime as she could to save the money. Meanwhile, she heard that there was an elderly missionary in China called Jeannie Lawson who needed a helper.

Eventually Gladys had enough money for the fare. She set off, ignoring warnings of a war between the Russians and the Chinese at the end of the line. At last, after a hazardous journey by a combination of ship, train, bus and mule, she reached the walled town of Yangcheng in the North China mountains where Mrs Lawson was working.

At first, the Chinese regarded the two strange English ladies as foreign devils. They threw mud at them and spat whenever they saw them. But Mrs Lawson and Gladys thought of a way of overcoming their hostility. They turned their home into an inn. Soon, they had a regular stream of customers from the mule trains which passed through the town, and became accepted by the local people.

When Mrs Lawson died, Gladys carried on alone at the inn. The local Mandarin also gave her a new job, as the area's foot inspector. Four years after she arrived in the country Gladys became a Chinese citizen.

In 1938 war broke out between China and Japan. Gladys organized relief work during the bombing of Yangcheng by the Japanese, and helped to get the people out of the city.

▲ Gladys with Jeannie Lawson, the missionary she came to help. When Mrs Lawson died, Gladys took over. She became known by the local people as Ai-weh-deh, 'the virtuous one'.

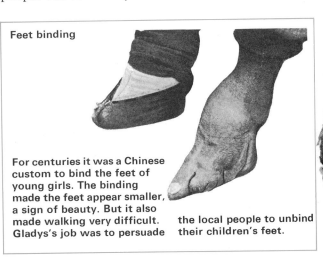

Feet binding

For centuries it was a Chinese custom to bind the feet of young girls. The binding made the feet appear smaller, a sign of beauty. But it also made walking very difficult. Gladys's job was to persuade the local people to unbind their children's feet.

▼ Gladys leading her charges on the long and arduous journey across the mountains to safety. The elder children had to help the younger ones constantly, often carrying them over more treacherous parts. The thin, home-made cloth shoes of the children soon became worn out, and their feet were cut and bleeding. Throughout the journey they were all desperately short of food and drink.

▼ Gladys tells a Bible story to the convicts in Yangcheng gaol. She gained their trust and once even succeeded in quelling a riot there.

When the fighting first began, Gladys felt that as a missionary she should not take sides. Later, she was persuaded that it was her duty to help save her adopted country. She used her knowledge of remote mountain villages and tracks to go behind the Japanese lines and give information to the Chinese soldiers.

Soon a reward was being offered for her capture. The local people had returned to Yangcheng, but the Japanese were advancing again. Gladys decided that the town was too dangerous, not only for her but for the large group of refugee children there. She would take them to Sian, a city in the plains beyond the mountains.

The journey to Sian was a nightmare. Gladys took nearly a hundred children, some only five years old. Somehow they survived the 12-day walk across steep and treacherous mountain tracks from Yangcheng to the Yellow River. Here they hoped for a boat, but for four days did not see one. They waited, with hardly any food, and in great danger from the Japanese.

At last they were spotted by a Chinese patrol and taken to the other side. They still had a difficult journey ahead, but eventually, thanks to her courage and determination, Gladys Aylward brought them safely to the end of their adventure.

In Search of the Past

Heinrich Schliemann: uncovering history

Heinrich Schliemann was a very imaginative child. When he was seven, he was given a Christmas present which shaped the course of his life. It was a copy of Dr Jerrer's *Universal History*, and in it was a picture of Troy in flames.

He already knew the legend which described how the Trojan Prince Paris had carried off Helen, the wife of the Spartan King Menelaus, and how the Greek heroes had gone to Troy to bring her back. The picture convinced Heinrich that Troy must really have existed. Somewhere, its ruins must be buried under the earth.

Schliemann's father was a poor clergyman, and Heinrich's early life was one of hardship. He was, however, exceptionally clever. He had to leave school at 14 to become apprenticed to a grocer. But before he was 30, he had amassed a huge fortune as a businessman, mostly in Russia and the United States.

He did not forget the picture of Troy in flames. He was determined to discover the remains of the ancient city, and he saw his money-making only as a means to this end.

When Schliemann began to dig for Troy at Hissarlik in Turkey, the experts shook their heads. Most scholars believed that the story of Troy related by Homer in the *Iliad* was pure myth. As one of them put it, looking for Troy was like looking for gold in the rays of the sun. Only a few people were prepared to accept that Troy had existed, and some of these thought the site lay to the south of Hissarlik, at a place called Bunarbishi. Schliemann was convinced that the landscape round Hissarlik fitted the descriptions which he had read time and time again in Homer's *Iliad*.

Excavating Hissarlik was not easy. The Turkish authorities were hostile to the enterprise, and did

▶ Heinrich Schliemann and (right) his wife Sophia. Schliemann wanted a wife who looked like the Helen of Troy of his imagination. So at the age of 47, he married Sophia Engastromenos, a 17-year-old girl from Athens. It was an arranged marriage, but as Sophia began to capture Heinrich's enthusiasm for Troy, they soon became a formidable partnership. In the photograph Sophia is wearing some of the jewellery they found together at Troy.

▼ The map shows the position of Troy and Mycenae.

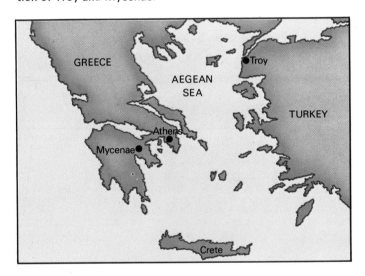

everything they could to obstruct it. Schliemann was also in constant danger of being attacked by the brigands who roamed the area.

Nevertheless he and his workers dug on. They were soon making discoveries, though in his enthusiasm, Schliemann dug straight through the walls of a later ancient settlement. He found several more layers of civilization underneath this, but after two years of excavations he felt sure he had found Homer's city of Troy.

When the next year he and his wife discovered a fabulous hoard of gold objects, he felt this confirmed his theory. The find was the most sensational archaeological discovery of the 19th century. Three years later, Schliemann caused another sensation. He discovered more treasure at Mycenae, the city of Agamemnon who had led the Greeks to Troy.

Later scholars have modified Schliemann's theories and criticised his methods. Few, however, have denied their debt to him for his unshakeable belief in the existence of Troy.

▼ It was a painting such as this one of Troy in flames which set Heinrich Schliemann off on his search for the remains of the ancient city.

▶ Within this grave circle at Mycenae, Schliemann discovered five Shaft Graves. These were royal tombs containing the bodies of 19 people. The bodies were laden with jewels and surrounded by many other beautiful objects. Schliemann was convinced that he had found the bodies of Agamemnon and his companions. In fact the Shaft Graves were dug about 200 years before the time of the Trojan War.

▼ Schliemann (centre) and some of his workers during the excavation of the royal grave circle.

▼ When Schliemann found this gold mask covering the face of a body in one of the shaft graves, he was sure he was gazing upon the face of Agamemnon.

Charles Darwin: the voyage of the *Beagle*

Charles Darwin did not seem to have a very exciting life ahead of him when in 1831 he left Cambridge University at the age of 22. He was planning to become a country parson. Yet, he was soon to set off on a great adventure which sent him travelling round the world for five years, and led him to make some of the most important scientific discoveries of the 19th century.

Darwin was very average at his studies, but he was an enthusiastic collector of all forms of wild life. A Cambridge professor who shared his enthusiasm recommended him for an unpaid job as a naturalist aboard *H.M.S. Beagle*, a small ship which was setting out to survey the South American coast. Darwin accepted.

As soon as the *Beagle* set sail, Darwin was terribly seasick. He spent much of the next five years aboard the ship, but went on feeling ill whenever she was at sea. Still, he was determined to go on.

The *Beagle* would be based at a particular port for quite long periods. This gave Darwin a chance to go ashore and explore. On several occasions in South America, Darwin found himself in the midst of civil wars and rebellions. However he refused to be put off from making his observations of wild life.

Soon Darwin was beginning to develop the ideas for which everybody remembers him. Before Darwin, people believed that what the Bible says about the Creation of the World was literally true. God made the earth on a single day. Two Victorian churchmen even worked out which day. They reckoned it was Sunday 23rd October, 4004 B.C. Everything on the earth was made in the next five days. On the seventh day, God rested.

As he travelled around, Darwin saw more and more aspects of nature which seemed to contradict the traditional view. At Punta Alta, he found the bones of some huge prehistoric monsters. Some of these were like animals of the present day, only much bigger.

▶ **The Galapagos Finches**

These small birds helped to lead Darwin to his theory of the origin of species. The finches vary greatly from one island to another, particularly in the shape of their beaks. What has happened is that, over thousands of years, the birds with features most suited to the food available on a particular island have flourished there, and those less well adapted have died out. Darwin called this process the survival of the fittest. It explains how the animals and man himself have evolved.

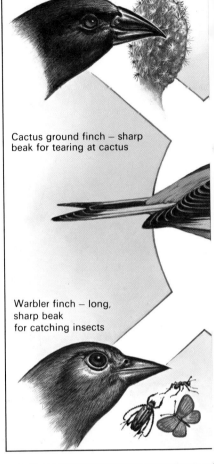

Cactus ground finch – sharp beak for tearing at cactus

Warbler finch – long, sharp beak for catching insects

▼ The *Beagle* laid ashore for repairs at the mouth of the River Santa Cruz near the tip of South America. Although he enjoyed life on board, Darwin welcomed any interruption of the voyage as a chance to go exploring.

▲ The land iguana, one of the strange creatures which have survived only in the Galapagos. Darwin found land iguanas over a metre in length. He learnt that they had sharp teeth, but were nevertheless harmless.

Tool-using finch

Ancestral finch

Large ground finch – strong beak for breaking nuts, seeds

Darwin wondered whether the sloth, the armadillo and the wild llama, for instance, were really part of the Creation. Could they not have developed over the centuries from the giant sloth, the giant armadillo and the giant wild llama whose bones he had found?

Above Valparaiso in Chile, Darwin found some fossilized seashells 4,000 metres up in the Andes. The rocks, he began to realize, must once have been at sea-level. The earth had changed since the Creation as well as the animals on it.

It was the visit to the Galapagos Islands which sparked off Darwin's ideas most of all. He was astonished by the number of varieties of each bird and mammal there. There were 15 different species of finch alone. Darwin realized that over many thousands of years the birds most suited to each island had survived and those which were less well adapted had become extinct.

Darwin took many years to work out the full details of his theory of the survival of the fittest. Eventually he realized that man, like the other animals, must be descended from something much more primitive. He came to believe that human beings are related to apes, sharing with them a common ancestor.

It was such a shocking idea in Victorian England that Darwin had a long battle to persuade people that he had discovered the truth. Yet Darwin's work on the voyage was an extraordinary achievement. Few thinkers can have travelled so far and endured so much to extend human knowledge.

▶ Like the land iguana, the Galapagos giant tortoise looks prehistoric. Darwin calculated it could travel up to 6 kilometres a day. He went for a ride on one, and his weight hardly slowed it down at all.

▼ While churchmen raged against Darwin's disbelief in the Book of Genesis, others made fun of him. This cartoon implied that, as far as Darwin himself was concerned, the ape was a rather recent ancestor.

Jane Goodall

Chimpanzees may seem familiar enough as the favourites in the zoo or the star performers in the circus. It is one thing, however, to train chimps to perform in captivity; it is quite another to find out how they behave in the wild. Little was known about the way man's closest relatives lived in their natural surroundings until a young woman set out in 1960 to study them at the Gombe Stream Resèrve on Lake Tanganyika in eastern Africa.

Jane Goodall did not have a university education but she was very interested in wild animals. She had been fascinated by chimpanzees ever since she was given a toy one as a child. Her enthusiasm so impressed the anthropologist Louis Leakey that he suggested she should take on a tremendous project.

The only person to have studied chimpanzees in the wild before had spent just two and a half months in the field. The thorough study which Leakey wanted would take at least two years. Also, the particular chimps he had in mind lived in a mountainous area of tropical forest cut off from civilization.

Jane Goodall had to put up with a great deal of hardship by the Gombe Stream. Conditions were primitive. She suffered from several attacks of fever. There were also dangerous wild animals in the neighbourhood and Jane had several frightening encounters with leopards and poisonous snakes. On one occasion when she was wading in the shallow waters of the lake, a 2-metre-long water cobra came so close that it touched her foot. Hardly daring to breathe, Jane waited until a wave had drawn the deadly snake away again and then leapt quickly out of the water.

▼ Jane Goodall is visited at her lakeside camp by some curious African children. Not all visitors were as welcome. Baboons would frequently invade the camp, scattering everything in sight and stealing precious food supplies. But it was a great thrill when, after about two years, the first chimps ventured into the camp for food.

▶ Chimpanzees resting in a tree in their dense tropical forest habitat.

▶ Chimp mothers have a great deal of physical contact with their young. When Jane Goodall had her own child, she followed the chimps' example and kissed and cuddled her son as much as possible.

Above all, the work was lonely. Jane Goodall had to work by herself, because she felt that one human being would be less likely to frighten the chimps than two or more. Luckily she had the patience to wait hour after hour, day after day, watching for them.

She was able to watch chimpanzees a few times during her first ten days in the Reserve, but then spent eight frustrating weeks seeing nothing. However she persevered. Gradually her patience was rewarded. She began to see more of the chimps, and in time they became used to her presence.

Soon she had made two exciting discoveries. One day she saw two chimpanzees in a tree with a pink object. To her surprise, it turned out to be meat from a piglet, which they were eating. Previously, scientists had thought that chimpanzees were vegetarians.

Then she stumbled on something even more exciting. She saw chimpanzees using grass stems as tools to prise insects out of the ground. One chimp stripped the leaves off a twig to make it the right shape. Scientists had believed that only men could make tools. Here was a chimpanzee proving them wrong.

Slowly, Jane Goodall began to know individual chimpanzees and to work out their relationships to one another. By painstaking observation over several years, she gained great insights into their behaviour. She realized how much there was to learn from them which would help in understanding man.

As time went by, Jane Goodall was joined by a team of research workers, who between them could document the life of the chimpanzee community around them for several years and in great detail. Without her lonely pioneering work, none of this would have been possible, and human knowledge would have been much the poorer.

Facial expressions

Jane Goodall learned how to interpret a wide variety of expressions on the faces of the chimpanzees which she studied.

1 The Display Face

Chimps look like this when they are being aggressive. Several times, Jane Goodall saw males charging at each other to demonstrate their strength.

2 The Play Face

Young chimps, like human children, play a great deal. This helps them to test out their surroundings. They find out, for instance, which branches will bear their weight and which will not. With the play face, they often make grunting or laughing sounds.

3 Pouting

Chimps use this expression when they are whimpering. A whimper sometimes follows the screams and squeaks of a young chimp who has been attacked. It can also be a sign of mounting frustration.

4 Pant-hoot

This is a call which a single chimp or a group of them will use to make contact with other chimps. They will use it, for example, when they reach a source of food and want to let other chimps know. It consists of a series of *hooo* sounds, which become louder, ending with *waaa* sounds.

5 Grinning

Chimps have several types of grins. The full closed grin here is the equivalent of a social or nervous smile by a human. It is accompanied by high-pitched squeaking.

◀ This chimp is using a twig as a tool to prise termites out of the ground.

Thor Heyerdahl: the *Kon-Tiki* expedition

August 3rd 1947 was the seventy-fifth birthday of King Haakon of Norway. On it, he received a message of congratulation from a most unusual source. It was sent by a small group of men floating on nine balsa logs in the middle of the Pacific.

The *Kon-Tiki* expedition sounded like a crazy idea. A Norwegian called Thor Heyerdahl was convinced that a tall white people who had settled in Polynesia about A.D. 500 had come there from Peru. He had discovered that there was a white king called Kon-Tiki in Inca legend who had sailed with his companions across the sea to the West. The Polynesians the other side of the Pacific talked of a white god called Tiki. The two, he thought, must be the same.

None of the experts believed Heyerdahl's theory. They said it was impossible for primitive people to sail so far. The only way Heyerdahl had of disproving them was to sail himself on a primitive raft from South America to Polynesia. He set out with five companions to Peru to build the *Kon-Tiki*.

People shook their heads. They said the *Kon-Tiki* could not be steered in high seas. They were sure the water would penetrate the balsa logs and sink them. Heyerdahl was confident.

The voyage went smoothly for the most part although there were some dramas. Once a whale shark, the largest fish known to man, started swimming round and round under the *Kon-Tiki*. It would have had the strength to capsize the raft without any trouble, but a well-aimed blow with a harpoon sent it away.

Later one of the men fell overboard. The *Kon-Tiki* could not turn round against the current to go back for him. In the nick of time another member of the crew swam out with a lifebelt and rescued him just before he fell too far behind the raft.

The most difficult part of the voyage was landing. Incredibly, the crew sighted the outermost Polynesian island in 93 days, less than the minimum time which they had reckoned for the voyage when they set off. However, winds and coral reefs made it impossible to land on the first two islands they passed. Eventually they ran aground on the Raroia coral reef. The raft was wrecked and the crew nearly drowned, but they had made it. From the reef, they could wade ashore in Polynesia, as Kon-Tiki himself perhaps had done. Thor Heyerdahl had proved not only that his theory was possible, but that with sufficient courage and luck, man can accomplish almost anything.

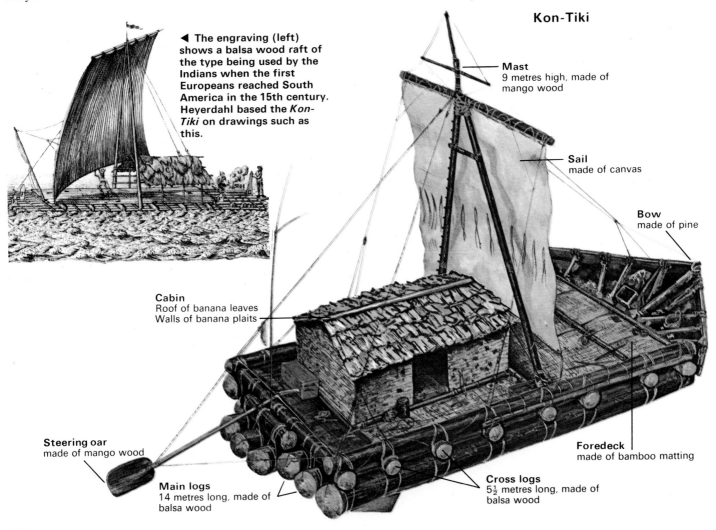

◄ The engraving (left) shows a balsa wood raft of the type being used by the Indians when the first Europeans reached South America in the 15th century. Heyerdahl based the *Kon-Tiki* on drawings such as this.

Kon-Tiki

Mast
9 metres high, made of mango wood

Sail
made of canvas

Bow
made of pine

Cabin
Roof of banana leaves
Walls of banana plaits

Foredeck
made of bamboo matting

Steering oar
made of mango wood

Main logs
14 metres long, made of balsa wood

Cross logs
5½ metres long, made of balsa wood

▲ Two of the impressive and mysterious statues found on Easter Island, an island halfway between the South American coast and the Polynesian Islands to which *Kon-Tiki* sailed. Heyerdahl believed that Easter Island too had been settled by Indians from Peru. He saw similarities between the Easter Island statues and some of the pre-Inca statues of the South American mainland.

The Ra expeditions

Thor Heyerdahl also crossed the Atlantic twice in reed boats. *Ra I* and *Ra II* were copies taken from ancient Egyptian paintings of boats made from the reed papyrus. There had been similar boats in ancient Peru. The pyramids in Mexico too were remarkably like the ones in Egypt. Could the Egyptians have possibly crossed the ocean and taken their knowledge of pyramids and reed boats with them? *Ra I*, built by Africans from Chad, sailed 4,500 kilometres before she had to be abandoned. *Ra II*, built by Bolivian Indians, completed the crossing from Morocco to Barbados with a crew of eight men from eight different countries.

▲ The *Kon-Tiki* proved surprisingly easy to handle once its crew mastered the technique. It rode the big waves without any trouble. Although the logs shifted about, they showed no signs of coming apart, even in the roughest weather.

▼ Food was no problem when Heyerdahl and his crew could catch fish such as this gold-finned tunny. Some smaller fish even landed on the raft in the night, providing the crew with an easy source of breakfast.

The Challenge of
the Elements

Pilâtre de Rozier: the first man to fly

According to 18th century theologians, God would not approve of ballooning. A man who went up in a balloon would be approaching the gates of Heaven before his proper time. King Louis XVI of France decided that, when the time came for the first manned balloon flight, the ascent should be made by a condemned criminal, of whom God would disapprove anyway.

Jean-François Pilâtre de Rozier, a young professor of physics and chemistry, argued against the King. The first flight would bring glory to France, and some of it would reflect on the man who attempted it. That man should not be a criminal. De Rozier suggested himself instead.

De Rozier was an associate of the Montgolfier brothers, who had launched the first unmanned balloon in public only four months before at Annonay. They had found that if you burned moist straw and wool, and enclosed the resulting gas in a light and air-tight covering, the covering would rise in the air.

That first ascent at Annonay started a mania for ballooning which swept first France and then the rest of Europe. Soon the Montgolfiers' rival, Professor Jacques Charles, had launched a balloon called *Globe*, filled with hydrogen. A huge crowd watched *Globe* rise in the air from the Champ de Mars in Paris.

De Rozier and the Montgolfiers went one better. They staged a flight for the King himself, and this time the balloon carried passengers. The first living beings to travel by air were a cock, a duck and a sheep. The flight was a success.

Now Pilâtre de Rozier, as test-pilot for the Montgolfiers, was ready to make a flight himself. He made two successful ascents in a balloon anchored to the ground by ropes. His first really spectacular feat, however, was a free flight, which he made with the Marquis François d'Arlandes.

▲ The first unmanned balloon launched by the Montgolfier brothers in June 1783.

▶ Pilâtre de Rozier and his companion take off their hats and bow to the crowd below during the first ever manned balloon flight.

▼ French villagers attack a landed balloon with pitchforks and guns. The first balloons were greeted with suspicion and fear by the people, who thought they were monsters.

Their balloon took off at 1.45 p.m. on 21st November 1783, in the presence of the Dauphin (the King's eldest son) and his courtiers. The balloonists carried a brazier below the balloon. By adding more fuel or damping the flames down they could control the quantity of gas the brazier produced to raise or lower their altitude. They went up to 900 metres and drifted 8 kilometres across Paris before landing.

De Rozier made several more flights during the next year. One of the most impressive was the ascent of *La Flesselles*, which carried seven people including de Rozier. A crowd of 60,000 gathered to watch, and the balloonists talked to them during the flight, through speaking trumpets. Despite a crash landing, the seven emerged unharmed. The same year de Rozier was chosen to pilot the King's own balloon, *Marie-Antoinette,* on its maiden voyage. Not long afterwards, however, the first aviator in history came to an untimely end when his balloon blew up over the Channel.

▶ The Montgolfier balloon was made of cane covered with paper-lined linen and coated with alum to reduce the fire risk.

framework of cane ———

outer covering of paper-lined linen ———

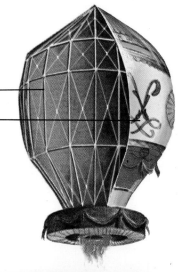

▼ De Rozier's *Aeromontgolfière* exploded over the Channel during an attempt to make the crossing from France to England. This bizarre double balloon had been a lethal combination of the Montgolfiers' fire balloon and Professor Charles' hydrogen balloon.

Amy Johnson: woman pioneer of aviation

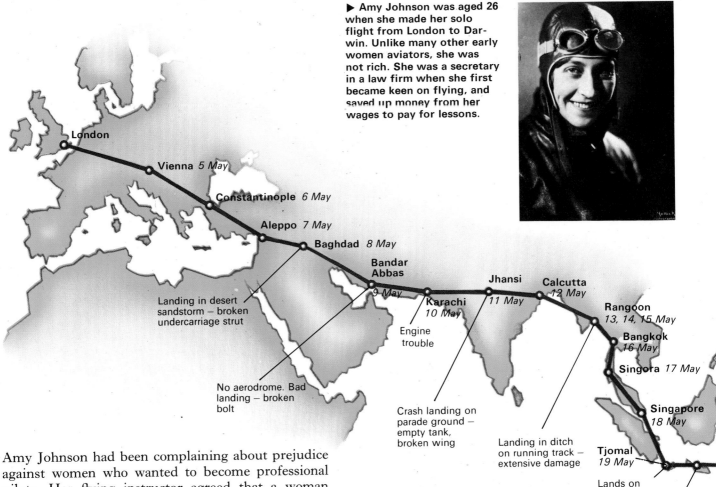

▶ Amy Johnson was aged 26 when she made her solo flight from London to Darwin. Unlike many other early women aviators, she was not rich. She was a secretary in a law firm when she first became keen on flying, and saved up money from her wages to pay for lessons.

London

Vienna *5 May*

Constantinople *6 May*

Aleppo *7 May*

Baghdad *8 May*

Bandar Abbas *9 May*

Karachi *10 May*

Jhansi *11 May*

Calcutta *12 May*

Rangoon *13, 14, 15 May*

Bangkok *16 May*

Singora *17 May*

Singapore *18 May*

Tjomal *19 May*

Sourabaya *20, 21 May*

Landing in desert sandstorm – broken undercarriage strut

No aerodrome. Bad landing – broken bolt

Engine trouble

Crash landing on parade ground – empty tank, broken wing

Landing in ditch on running track – extensive damage

Lands on building site

Amy Johnson had been complaining about prejudice against women who wanted to become professional pilots. Her flying instructor agreed that a woman would have to find a way of proving herself. Amy asked how. 'Oh, by flying to Australia, for instance', came the reply. The suggestion was not made seriously, but Amy immediately took up the challenge.

Strangely enough, Amy had not at first shown outstanding promise as a pilot. It was on the ground that she was exceptional. She had given up her secretarial job to train as an engineer. In December 1929, she became the first woman to be granted a ground engineer's licence by the Air Ministry.

The next month, she told a newspaper reporter that she was planning to fly solo to Australia. She spent an anxious time finding a sponsor to put up the money. Eventually, her perseverance paid off. Early in the morning of the 5th May 1930, she climbed into the cockpit of the de Havilland Gypsy Moth which she had called *Jason*. She was off.

Her journey required great courage and stamina. She would fly every day from sunrise until sunset, and then spend hours at her destination overhauling the plane. With very little sleep each night, she had to concentrate every second she was in the air on two things at once, navigating and flying the plane. *Jason* had a noisy engine which produced strong fumes. The flight was anything but comfortable.

Amy Johnson was hoping to beat the record of $15\frac{1}{2}$ days set by Bert Hinkler. This Australian pilot had made the first solo flight from England to Australia two years before. At first, it looked as if Amy would succeed. She reached Karachi, Pakistan, in two days less than Hinkler had done.

So far, there had been only minor mishaps. The second half of the journey was more hazardous. At Rangoon in Burma, she was supposed to land on the race course. She could not find it. She was almost out of fuel, and the largest space which she could see was a playing field. It proved too short, and Amy ended up in a ditch.

Somehow, the necessary repairs were carried out in three days. Luckily, there was a stock of shirts nearby which had been made out of war-surplus aeroplane fabric. The material could be reconverted to patch up *Jason*'s wings.

Amy eventually reached Darwin in 19 days. She had failed to beat Hinkler's record, but she had flown solo further than any woman before her. Her pioneering achievement made her a household name.

De Havilland Gypsy Moth DH 606

Amy called her plan *Jason*. She bought it for £600. It was two years old when she got it, and already equipped with special long-distance petrol tanks.

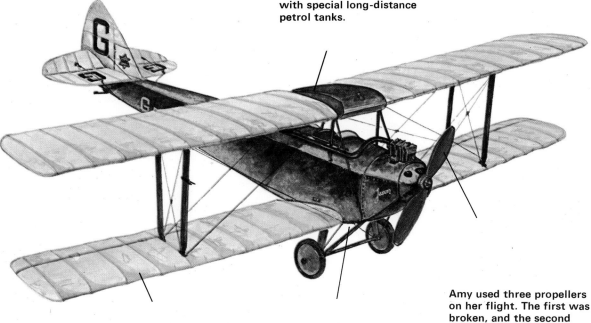

Amy used three propellers on her flight. The first was broken, and the second damaged by monsoon rains.

Jason's wings needed many repairs. By the end, Amy was having to use sticking plaster to mend them.

Jason's heavy fuel-tanks made taking off difficult. Amy only left the ground from London on her second attempt. Once in the air she had to keep pumping petrol by hand into the gravity tank in the upper wing – a smelly and unpleasant chore.

Lands between 2-metre-high anthills

Atamboea *22, 23 May*
Darwin *24 May*

AUSTRALIA

Melbourne

▶ The crowds cheer Amy in Melbourne. At the end of her flight, she spent six weeks touring Australia. She was treated as a heroine. There were huge crowds everywhere to greet her, and songs and poems were written about her flight. She found the tour exhausting, but she had to face many more tumultuous welcomes when she returned home to Britain.

Francis Chichester: voyage round the world

It was a beautiful Sunday evening in May 1967 when Francis Chichester came home to Plymouth. Half a million people were waiting there. Guns were fired. The beacon was lit on Drake's Island. At the age of 65, Chichester had sailed single-handed around the world. It was the climax of an extraordinary life of adventure.

As a young man, Chichester had tried to fly alone around the world. The attempt came to a sudden end, however, when he flew into some inconvenient telephone wires at a place called Katsuura in Japan.

Thirty-five years later, having survived lung cancer, he was off again, this time by boat. He had already won the first transatlantic race for solo yachtsmen in his boat *Gipsy Moth III*, named after his plane. Now he had a new *Gipsy Moth*, stronger and faster, but harder work to handle.

Many had sailed round the world before him. But Chichester saw the chance of doing it faster than any other small boat, by calling in at only one port, Sydney in Australia. He also planned to take the dangerous route around Cape Horn on the southern tip of South America.

A single-hander has too many jobs to tackle to have much time to feel lonely. Domestic chores like cooking and washing have to be fitted in with sail-changing, navigation and repairs. Despite the aid of his self-steering gear which allowed him to leave the boat to steer itself, Chichester seldom had a full night's sleep with no interruptions.

▲ *Gipsy Moth IV* rounds Cape Horn. Nine people had attempted this in small yachts before Chichester, and six of them had capsized. The waves there can reach 30 metres high, and Chichester had to cope with winds at up to 160 kilometres an hour. He admitted that he was frightened for a while.

▶ Sail plan of *Gipsy Moth IV*. Among the sails most frequently used were (1) the big genoa (55 square metres), (2) the trysail (13 square metres) and (3) the mizzen (13 square metres).

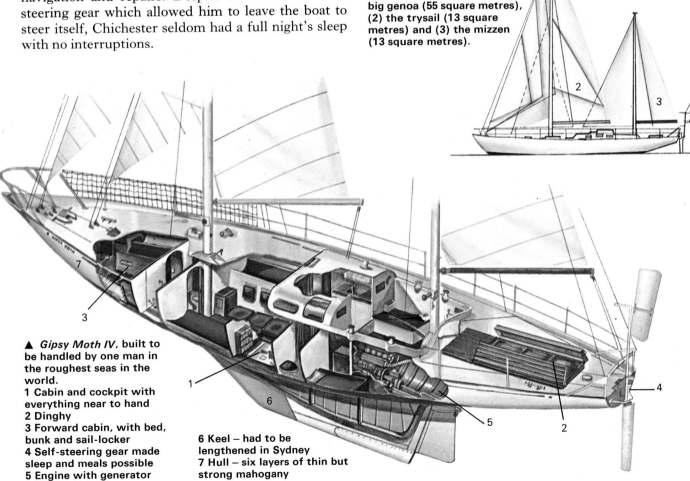

▲ *Gipsy Moth IV*, built to be handled by one man in the roughest seas in the world.
1 Cabin and cockpit with everything near to hand
2 Dinghy
3 Forward cabin, with bed, bunk and sail-locker
4 Self-steering gear made sleep and meals possible
5 Engine with generator
6 Keel – had to be lengthened in Sydney
7 Hull – six layers of thin but strong mahogany

With nearly 4,000 kilometres still to go to Sydney, the self-steering gear broke. At first, Chichester thought he would have to give up and head for the nearest port, Fremantle. Even that was over 1,500 kilometres away. Patiently, he experimented with an improvised steering sail, which proved so successful that he was able to change course again and continue on his way towards Sydney.

Chichester spent only seven weeks in Australia while *Gipsy Moth* was refitted for the second half of the voyage. A day out of Sydney on the way home, the boat capsized. The damage was considerable. A big sail had gone overboard, and large quantities of water had to be pumped out of the bottom of the boat. Stores and gear were jumbled up in an appalling mess in the cabin. There were clothes in the basin, vitamin pills scattered in all directions, and butter everywhere. Gradually, Chichester cleared up and sailed on his way.

Chichester reached Plymouth 119 days after leaving Sydney. He had taken half the time of the previous fastest voyage round the world in a small vessel. He had doubled the record for the longest passage without calling into port by a lone yachtsman. And he had achieved a new speed record for a single-hander by sailing 2,240 kilometres in eight days.

In July 1967 Queen Elizabeth II knighted Francis Chichester at Greenwich. She used the sword with which Queen Elizabeth I had knighted Francis Drake, a fitting gesture for possibly the greatest seaman of the second Elizabethan Age.

Clipper routes
For his round-world trip Chichester chose to sail along the Clipper Way, the route which the clipper captains had pioneered over the years. The clippers were the fastest commercial sailing ships which ever put to sea. The great tea clippers of the late 19th century, *Thermopylae* and *Cutty Sark*, achieved records for the England-Australia round trip which have never been broken. Chichester with his small boat and his crew of one, managed to keep up with their average time. In Australia, the Governor-General gave him three bales of wool, which he carried back in what he called 'the smallest wool clipper that ever left Australia'.

▲ Chichester winches the mizzen. Sails had to be changed frequently, sometimes as often as 13 times a day. Too little sail, and the wind was wasted; too much, and *Gipsy Moth* could capsize.

◀ *Gipsy Moth's* cabin at an angle, or heel, of 35°. Chichester once spent eight days continuously heeled over like this. He had a table (1) and chair (2) on a swinging balance to make it easier to work in such difficult conditions. Saucepans (3) and plates (4) were also firmly secured. There were problems, however. The contents of drawers and cupboards would frequently spill out over the floor. Next to the chair, there was a Primus stove (5) with a small oven. Chichester often had to interrupt his meals for urgent work in the boat, but he sometimes managed to cook himself a feast.

Jacques Cousteau: the depths revealed

Jacques Cousteau stood upside down on one finger and burst out laughing. He had done it. He had become a manfish, a human being who could move through the water with the freedom of a fish and without having to come up for air. His new invention, the aqualung, meant that divers were at last free from the dangerous and cumbersome helmets which had restricted them up to now.

That first aqualung dive in June 1943 opened up a whole new world of adventure under the water. Jacques Cousteau has been exploring, filming and experimenting with that world ever since.

Cousteau's early dives with his aqualung were often dangerous. Once his newly formed Undersea Research Group undertook to solve the mystery of the Fountain of Vaucluse. The Fountain, near Avignon in the south of France, is a pool in a crater above a river. Most of the time the water trickles gently out of it into the river, but, for five weeks in the year, the trickle becomes a torrent. Cousteau's mission was to find out why.

He went down with a diving partner, Frédéric Dumas. Sixty metres down, in an underwater tunnel, they lost their way. They had been misled by a fanciful description of the cave given by a man who had tried to explore it with a diving helmet ten years before. To make matters worse, the new air compressor which they had used to fill their cylinders was faulty. It had pumped in particles of the poisonous carbon monoxide gas from its engine.

▲ A diver making friends with a 'monster' of the deep.

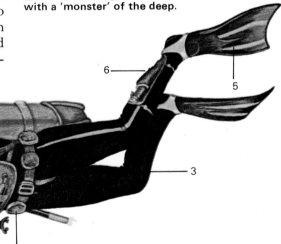

▲ Jacques Cousteau in his diving gear.

▲ A diver wearing the aqualung invented by Cousteau. Other accessories are:
1 Mask – underwater you can see little without one
2 Tank, with a regulator which delivers air whenever the diver breathes in
3 Wet suit – the body will lose heat fast in water if it is not protected
4 Weight belt to balance the buoyancy of the tank
5 Fins to improve speed
6 All-purpose knife
7 Waterproof watch
8 Flashlight

In the stupor caused by the gas, Dumas let go of the guideline, which would take them back to the entrance to the tunnel and then to the surface. Cousteau too was nearly overcome, and they risked an appalling death.

At last Cousteau found the line, but their troubles were not over. Dumas's diving suit was waterlogged. Cousteau could not swim to the surface supporting his companion's weight. He had to climb hand over hand up the rope. However, three tugs on the rope was an agreed signal to a man on the surface to pay out more rope. Every time Cousteau tried to climb up, the rope was let down. Just in time, the man at the surface realized that something was wrong. Cousteau and Dumas were hauled to safety. They had not solved the mystery of the Fountain but they were at least still alive.

▲ Cousteau's technology opened up a world of astonishing beauty, as shown by this coral reef in the Indian Ocean.

▶ Conshelf III

Cousteau has also developed sea habitats where divers can live for a considerable time under water at greater depths than are possible with the aqualung. In 1965, six occupants spent three weeks on the bed of the Mediterranean on Conshelf (Continental Shelf Station) Three. 100 metres down, they studied whether plant life could survive under artificial light on the dark seabed.

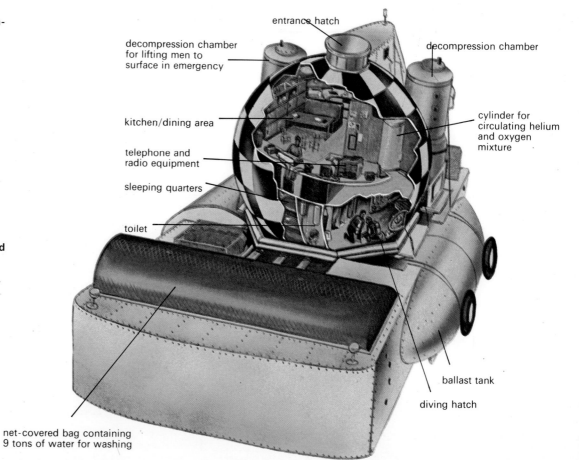

entrance hatch

decompression chamber for lifting men to surface in emergency

decompression chamber

kitchen/dining area

cylinder for circulating helium and oxygen mixture

telephone and radio equipment

sleeping quarters

toilet

ballast tank

diving hatch

net-covered bag containing 9 tons of water for washing

Tenzing Norgay: conqueror of Everest

In the Sherpa language, *Chomolungma* means 'the mountain so high no bird can fly over it'. That is what the Sherpa people of the Himalayas call Everest, the great mountain which looms over their homeland.

Tenzing Norgay has known Everest all his life. As a boy, he tended his father's yaks on its lower slopes. He could easily have spent the rest of his life looking after yaks, but he was restless to see more of the outside world. At the age of 18 he ran away from home. He had heard that there was to be a British expedition up Everest and the climber Hugh Ruttledge was recruiting Sherpas as porters.

The Sherpa people are naturally strong, and their lungs are used to breathing the thin air which exists at great heights. European mountaineers who have climbed in the Himalayas have always chosen Sherpas to carry their equipment.

Tenzing was desperate to be chosen for the Ruttledge expedition, but he was considered too young and inexperienced. Two years later, however, he was chosen by Eric Shipton as a porter on the fifth British Everest expedition. This was just to be a reconnaissance, but, for the Sherpas, there was still a great deal of hard work to do, carrying loads of up to 40 kilos. But Tenzing was disappointed when the expedition turned back. He wanted to reach the summit.

As the years went by, Tenzing became a very experienced climber. He took part in further attempts on Everest, and climbed with expeditions up the other massive mountains in the Himalayas. In time, he became a head Sherpa, or sirdar, with the job of organizing all the other porters on an expedition.

It was as sirdar that Tenzing went on the Swiss expedition to Everest of 1952, but the Swiss made him a full climbing member of the party as well and treated him as an equal. Until recently, the attempts had always started from Tibet to the north. Now the Nepali government was prepared to allow climbers to start from their territory to the south.

▲ Tenzing standing on the top of the world with the flags of Britain, Nepal, India and the United Nations tied to his axe.

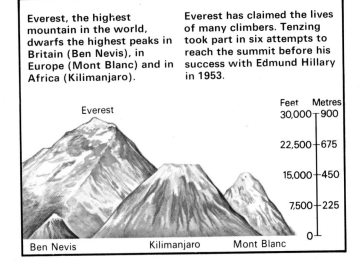

Everest, the highest mountain in the world, dwarfs the highest peaks in Britain (Ben Nevis), in Europe (Mont Blanc) and in Africa (Kilimanjaro).

Everest has claimed the lives of many climbers. Tenzing took part in six attempts to reach the summit before his success with Edmund Hillary in 1953.

	Feet	Metres
	30,000	900
	22,500	675
	15,000	450
	7,500	225
	0	

Everest

Ben Nevis   Kilimanjaro   Mont Blanc

The Swiss expedition climbed higher up Everest than any had before. Tenzing and a climber called Raymond Lambert made the final attempt on the summit. At their highest camp, they had to slap and rub each other all night to stop themselves freezing to death. They were defeated not far from the top.

It was left to a British party the following year to conquer Everest. Again Tenzing was both sirdar and full climber. He had been very ill during the previous winter but he did not allow that to stop him.

This time, the weather was better for the final ascent. Hillary and Tenzing conquered the last treacherous rocks. At 11.30 on the morning of 29th May 1953, they shook hands at the highest point in the world. Tenzing Norgay, the son of the yak-herder, had conquered Chomolungma.

◄ Tenzing and Hillary enjoy a brief rest before attacking the last stage of their climb. An advance party cut steps in the ice to save their energies for the final assault. At these altitudes breathing in the thin air was a problem and even Tenzing had to resort to using an oxygen mask. Thirst too was a big problem at this height. To obtain water the climbers had to melt snow and ice.

▼ Approach by rope ladder to Camp Three. Ladders were used on the more treacherous slopes to make the climb easier for those who were carrying loads from one camp to the next. Hillary and Tenzing made many trips up and down the lower part of the mountain to carry light loads and to train for the attempt on the summit. They learned to work as a team.

Summit
29 May
8850 metres

South Summit

Camp 9
8600 metres

Camp 8
8000 metres

Camp 7
7300 metres

Camp 6
6900 metres

Camp 4
6400 metres

Camp 5
6700 metres

Camp 3
6000 metres

Camp 2
5900 metres

2nd Base Camp
12 April
5480 metres

◄ There were nine camps on the route up Everest. From the base camp teams were organized to cut a route to the higher camps and to carry up loads. Only two men reached the summit, but they depended on the work of hundreds of others.

▶ Crossing a crevasse below Camp Two. Hillary once fell into a crevasse like this. Luckily, he was roped to Tenzing, who managed to stop him falling too far and to pull him up.

Impressions of Adventure

Mark Twain: from Mississippi pilot to writer

Mark Twain thought he had struck it rich. With his partner he had established a claim on a silver mine worth a million dollars. All they had to do was a little digging within ten days, and the mine was theirs. Somehow, each of them was convinced that the other was doing the work. When, ten days later, the mine had still not been touched, they lost all rights to it.

Mark Twain's life was full of dramatic ups and downs like that. His own adventures provided more than enough stories for his books.

His real name was Sam Clemens. He was born in poverty, but he was always dreaming of better things. After working for a while as a printer, he set off to seek his fortune in South America. On the boat trip down to New Orleans, he decided to stay on the river instead. He worked as a pilot on the great steamboats which plied up and down the Mississippi.

When the American Civil War broke out in 1861, traffic on the river came to a standstill. Sam Clemens headed out West by stage coach to Nevada with his brother. In the Rocky Mountains, he met the notorious murderer Slade, who had killed 26 people, in some cases sending the ears of his victims to their relatives. Sam found him very charming and hospitable, though he was nervous when Slade insisted on giving him the last cup of coffee at breakfast. 'I could not feel sure that he would not be sorry, presently, that he had given it away', he wrote, 'and proceed to kill me to distract his thoughts from the loss'.

Sam did not find the fortune at the end of the trail for which he had hoped. He discovered a wealth of experience for his book *Roughing It*, but not the silver for which he was looking.

▲ Huckleberry Finn, the character based on the son of the village drunkard in Hannibal, where Twain grew up.

▲ Mark Twain. His pen name is either a pilot's term for two fathoms or a barman's for two drinks on credit.

▶ Steamboats on the River Mississippi. Mark Twain worked on boats like these for nearly four years. He wrote, 'I loved the profession far better than any I have followed since'.

▼ Tom Sawyer, the hero of Mark Twain's famous book, tricks the village boys into whitewashing his aunt's fence. Tom was given the job as a punishment, but he pretended it was a great honour. 'It's got to be done very careful; I reckon there ain't one boy in a thousand, maybe two thousand, that can do it the way it's got to be done'. The boys end up paying Tom for a turn with the brush.

▲ Huckleberry Finn and his friend Jim, a Negro slave, drifting down the Mississippi in their bid for freedom. 'We said there warn't no home like a raft, after all. Other places do seem so cramped up and smothery, but a raft don't. You feel mighty free and easy and comfortable on a raft'. As a boy, Twain had played beside the river and ridden the giant log rafts which drifted down it.

His Nevada was peopled by characters larger than life. There was the drunk with the cork leg, for instance, who pretended when someone dropped something on his foot that the pain was so intense that only large quantities of brandy could cure it.

Clemens' failure at silver-mining, however, caused him to turn to the career which made his name. He started writing for newspapers. Soon he was using the name Mark Twain. From journalist, he turned to author. A tour of Europe and the Middle East inspired *The Innocents Abroad*, a book which created a lasting picture of the rich American tourist.

But Twain returned to the experiences of his childhood on the Mississippi to create the two works for which he is most remembered, *Tom Sawyer* and *Huckleberry Finn*. However, the fame which these brought did not make him any less restless. He became involved in the development of an automatic typesetting machine but the project drove him to bankruptcy. He won back his fortune by lecturing around the world and writing a book about his experiences called *Following the Equator*.

Paul Gauguin: artist in Tahiti

The adventures of Paul Gauguin's life probably started with the vases and little statues he saw about the house when he was a child. They were primitive works, made by Indians in Peru and brought back from there by his mother. They were the starting point of his fascination for primitive things. The yearning to find a simpler way of life was to drive Gauguin to travel to more and more remote places, and to inspire him to change the history of art with his impressions of what he saw and felt about them.

Gauguin waited until he was 35 years old before he started in earnest on his life's work. He had been rich and successful in a career which gave him little satisfaction. He had taken up painting as a hobby. Suddenly he announced to his wife 'From now on I paint every day'.

Soon, he began the long search for unspoilt surroundings, where he could feel at peace with the world and best convey the vividness of nature in his art. In Pont-Aven in Brittany, he began to develop his own distinctive style of painting. He started to exaggerate the brightness of colours and the basic shapes in his pictures, leaving out unnecessary detail to portray the mood of a scene most dramatically.

Gauguin's new life meant much sacrifice. He had left his wife and family, and he soon ran out of money.

He went out to Panama, hoping to earn enough digging the canal there to keep going for several months afterwards as a painter. The conditions for canal workers were appalling. Gauguin left for Martinique, where the tropical surroundings suited him ideally. However, he fell ill, spent all his cash and had to work his way home as a sailor.

▲ *Harvest in Brittany*, one of Gauguin's early works. His first attempts to find a more natural way of life took him to the more primitive parts of France. He even took to wearing Breton dress and clogs.

▶ A detail taken from *Faa Iheihe*, another of Gauguin's South Sea paintings. As in so many of his works of this period, beautiful native women and luxurious vegetation are a major source of inspiration.

Soon, he decided to turn his back on Western civilization for ever and go to Tahiti. The island had just become a French colony, but Gauguin did not live as the colonial settlers did. He had a native hut, and he always took the side of the local people in any dispute they had with the authorities. In due course he married a native girl.

After two years, he was driven back to France by poverty and illness. An exhibition of his work was a failure; he was too far ahead of his time. He had more quarrels too with his first wife about money.

Eventually he was able to return to the South Seas. During this period he produced some wonderful paintings, often drawing on local myths for inspiration. He had become very involved in Polynesian beliefs and had frequent quarrels with the missionaries.

When Gauguin died at the age of 55 in his wooden house in the Marquesas Islands, his genius was at last beginning to be recognized in France.

William Russell

The young officers at the Crimean battlefront called Billy Russell a jolly good fellow. Queen Victoria's husband Prince Albert described him as 'that miserable scribbler'. A former Secretary for War suggested he should be executed. Russell was the kind of man who provoked strong reactions in people.

Before the Crimean War, there had been no such thing as a professional war correspondent. Newspapers relied on accounts written by officers serving in the field. It was not surprising that their reports often took a long time to arrive, and that they contained only the most extravagant praise for the army.

When Britain and France declared war on Russia in 1854, the British public had a great appetite for news of glorious British deeds against the enemy. The editor of *The Times* decided that he needed a correspondent of his own on the spot. William Howard Russell, a tough and enterprising Irishman, was given the job.

The army was not sure how to react to Russell's presence. They certainly did not take to him when he started describing what was going on in the camp. *The Times* had reported when the British expedition set off that it was 'the finest army that has ever left these shores'. In fact, the forces were under the command of a group of aristocratic officers who had little experience in the battlefield. Their military ideas were hopelessly old-fashioned. The organization of supplies and medical treatment was chaotic. Russell spared the readers of *The Times* few details of the incompetence which he saw all around him.

The Commander-in-Chief, Lord Raglan, decided that Russell was to have no help or food from the army. He lost most of his clothes; when he pitched his tent alongside those of the troops, it was cut down. However, Russell was good at looking after himself.

▲ This painting, entitled 'The Thin Red Line', shows the stand of the 93rd Highland Regiment against the Russian Cavalry at the Battle of Balaclava. Russell himself first described the Highlanders in one of his dispatches as a 'thin red streak topped with steel'. His phrase was adapted to 'the thin red line', and became a symbol for British gallantry against heavy odds.

◀ Russell made himself very unpopular by his outspoken reports of mismanagement of the Crimean War. He was largely responsible for the fall from power of the Prime Minister of the time, Lord Aberdeen.

The 'scoop' that misfired

Before the telegraph was invented, reporters went to great lengths to get news back to their newspapers before their rivals.

In 1884 an Irish statesman, Daniel O'Connell, was on trial in Dublin. Russell heard the verdict of guilty.

He immediately took a carriage to the station.

He caught a special train from Dublin to Kingston, where the *Iron Duke*, a steamboat specially chartered for *The Times*, was waiting for him.

Despite the hostility, Russell stayed with the army throughout the war. At the Battle of the Alma, he rode up and down behind the lines, questioning as many participants as he could find about what was going on. His dispatches were read eagerly by the public back home. His account of the heroism involved in an appalling military blunder, the Charge of the Light Brigade, helped to make it the most famous episode of the war.

Russell's later career took him all over the world, wherever there was fighting. He covered the Indian Mutiny, the American Civil War, the Franco-Prussian War and the Zulu War of 1879 in South Africa. As a new generation of correspondents emerged, familiar with the recently invented telegraph, Russell's techniques became rather out of date. However, he had pioneered a new form of journalism that lives on today.

◀ A bleak winter scene in the Crimea. On the left Russell is sitting in his tent writing up a dispatch. In the centre is Florence Nightingale. Florence had read Russell's reports of the appalling conditions in the Crimea. She left England in October 1854 to nurse the sick and wounded. The winter of 1854—55 was a nightmare. The troops were in rags and desperately short of food. Diseases spread like wildfire through the camps. In vast filthy buildings with few medical supplies, Florence and her nurses worked day and night to make life as tolerable as possible for the wretched soldiers in their care.

The *Iron Duke* took him full steam ahead to Holyhead in Wales.

From Holyhead Russell caught another special train to London. During the journey he took off his boots and slept. He caught a cab at Euston, but only managed to put one boot back on.

He ran into *The Times* office with the other boot under his arm. A man at the door, whom Russell took to be a printer, asked him the verdict. Unfortunately, he was a spy posed by the rival *London Herald*! The next day the story appeared in both papers!

Herbert Ponting: Antarctic photographer

Herbert Ponting was one of the great pioneers of photography. Although he travelled all over the world, his most famous pictures were all taken on the same journey, the expedition of Captain Robert Scott to the Antarctic.

By 1909, when Scott was planning his expedition, Ponting was already a well-known photographer. Scott was very keen that there should be a complete pictorial record of his expedition. Ponting enthusiastically accepted the job of official photographer.

Cine-photography was just beginning at the time. Ponting decided to learn how to use a movie camera so that he could film in the Antarctic. Taking photographs in the icy conditions posed many problems. To thread film into his camera, Ponting had to take off his gloves and risk getting frostbite as his bare fingers touched the metal of the camera. He had only to breathe on a lens in the open air for it to become unusable. Developing film too was a tedious and tricky business in such cold temperatures. But Ponting was undaunted and spent many hours in his elaborate darkroom while the other members of the party were sleeping.

Like many artists, Ponting was obsessed by his art, and was unwilling to let anything interfere with it. He caused some bad feeling among other members of the expedition by refusing to share chores like unloading the ship. Many people would claim, however, that the photographs which he took justified his single-mindedness.

He was also prepared to go to extraordinary lengths to obtain the pictures. Soon after their ship the *Terra Nova* landed, Scott told him he had sighted some killer whales. The whales dived into the sea and Ponting ran with his camera to the place where he thought they would surface again. The whales actually came up right under him. Luckily they knocked him backwards onto the ice instead of forwards into the sea. Even so, the piece of ice on which he was standing was now adrift. He was too far from the solid ice to jump and the whales were a few yards behind him. Luckily, the current suddenly pushed the ice floe in a different direction, and he was able to scramble to safety.

When the winter ended, Scott was planning to take a team to the South Pole. Ponting spent hours teaching members of this polar party how to take photographs. As a result, his pupils were able to leave a pictorial record of the journey from which they were never to return.

Ponting ran his movie camera as the party set off for the Pole. His film was first shown back in England a few weeks before Scott and his companions died.

For the rest of his life, Ponting remained obsessed by the tragic expedition. His last years were mainly taken up with unsuccessful attempts to promote the unique film he had made. They made a sad contrast with the pioneering achievements of his earlier life.

▲ Ponting at work photographing the wildlife of Antarctica, a favourite subject.

◄ Some of Ponting's most spectacular shots were taken on board the ship *Terra Nova* as it crashed through the ice floes. He fixed the camera on the end of some planks jutting 3 metres out from the deck, and clung onto these planks himself to operate it as the ship cut its way through the ice.

▼▶ *A grotto in an iceberg* (right) and *The death of an iceberg* (below), two of Ponting's greatest photographs.

Challenges of the past and future

When Sebastian Cabot was hired by King Edward VI as Grand Pilot of England in 1551, he was named 'Governour of the mysterie and companie of the merchants adventurers for the discoverie of regions, dominions, islands and places unknowen'. Today there might appear to be no mystery left in the world, no adventure to be had and no regions remaining to be discovered.

Yet the history of exploration is not a simple story of Europeans slowly expanding the frontiers of their world until they knew everything there was to know about everywhere. In fact, during the great age of discovery in the 15th and 16th centuries, European explorers depended heavily on knowledge gained by the Arab merchant seamen, who were the great travellers of the Middle Ages. Many of the new places the Europeans found may well have been discovered before in more ancient times.

Many discoveries were made through errors which slowly led to the truth. Columbus, for example, thought he could find a way to the Indies by sailing west. He found America instead.

▲ The world map of the Arab al-Idrisi, 1154. He thought that the world was flat and measured 36,640 kilometres around the edge. The water surrounding the earth, according to al-Idrisi, held it 'stable in space like the yolk of an egg'. The south is at the top, so that the Indian Ocean is shown above the Mediterranean. Some early European maps, like the one completed by Fra Mauro in 1459, also show the world this way up.

◀ The earth photographed from space, showing clearly the landmass of Africa. In the 20th century, man has been made all too aware of the limits of our planet and of its resources. In 'The Ra Expeditions', Thor Heyerdahl describes his thoughts as he looked back at the sea at the end of the voyage. He writes of the ocean lying 'seemingly boundless, as in Columbus' day'. He goes on to wonder whether man would abandon his war against nature. 'Would future generations restore early man's respect and veneration for the sea and the earth, humbly worshipped by the Inca as . . . Mother-Sea and Mother-Earth?'.

▲ In 1974, John Blashford-Snell led the first expedition to complete a full navigation of the Zaire River. The expedition took four months, and covered 3,148 kilometres of swamp river and jungle. The team of soldiers, scientists and civilian explorers travelled by inflatable rubber boat. They collected specimens for research on medicine, zoology and botany. Among the problems they faced were tropical diseases and rapids which were uncharted by man.

▶ Wally Herbert took 476 days to cross the Arctic from Alaska to Spitzbergen. With his three companions and his dogs, he travelled 5,800 kilometres across the ice. The journey was over constantly shifting ice floes. The movement of the ice put the expedition off course and behind time. They spent the long dark Arctic winter short of the North Pole. They then had to drive themselves to the limit to reach their goal before warmer weather made further progress impossible.

Later explorers with a more scientific turn of mind uncovered the mysteries of Australasia, the African interior and the Antarctic. Soon, steamships, trains, cars and aeroplanes brought them within the reach of ordinary people.

Yet there *is* something left for explorers of the present day. Wally Herbert, who made an epic journey across the Arctic in 1969, gave as his reason for going that only one pioneer journey was left to man on the surface of the earth – a journey across the top of the world. However, John Blashford-Snell, who led the conquest of the Ethiopian Blue Nile and the Zaire River expedition of 1974, has shown that there is still some scope for a pioneer explorer.

The challenge of the elements remains as well. Space flight may involve too much technology and too much team effort to satisfy the true pioneering spirit, but the Americans who tried to cross the Atlantic by balloon in 1977 were genuine heirs to de Rozier.

John Fairfax, too, who rowed across the Atlantic in 1969 showed that there were still new ways to prove man's powers of endurance. It took him 180 days to row from the Canary Islands to Florida, U.S.A. Despite a leg injury and frequent sickness, he kept going, often rowing for 12 hours a day.

The past offers as many challenges as ever. If men have abandoned the search for El Dorado, they are still arguing about another ancient lost city, Atlantis. With some of the luck of a Heinrich Schliemann to help him, the Greek Professor Marinatos discovered in 1967 a magnificent palace on the island of Thera which provided some powerful clues to the mystery.

But perhaps the greatest challenge is of the future itself. Pioneers like Heyerdahl and Cousteau stress how vulnerable our planet is to exploitation by man. The future of pioneering may lie in the quest to understand nature better through its wilder, less spoilt regions, and to learn how to conserve its resources.

How to find out more

BOOKS TO READ

The Odyssey by Homer, translated by E. V. Rieu
(Penguin)

East and West

A History of Discovery and Exploration (Aldus Books/
Jupiter Books, London) in 5 volumes:
1) *The Search Begins*
2) *The New World*
3) *Eastern Island, Southern Seas*
4) *Africa and Asia : Mapping Two Continents*
5) *Earth's Last Frontiers*
Genghis Khan and the Mongols by Michael Gibson
(Wayland)
Sir Walter Ralegh by John Winton (Michael Joseph)
The Incas by Barbara Beck (Franklin Watts)
The Aztecs by Barbara Beck (Franklin Watts)
The Devil Drives : a life of Sir Richard Burton by Fawn
Brodie (Penguin)
Mary Kingsley's Travels in West Africa, edited by
R. Glynn Grylls (Knight)
The Explorers by Desmond Wilcox (BBC Publications)
Lawrence of Arabia by Sarah Sayer (Wayland)
The Small Woman (the life of Gladys Aylward) by Alan
Burgess (Evans)

In Search of the Past

Men of Archaeology by Katherine Shippen (Dobson)
Lost Civilizations by Leonard Cottrell (Collins/Franklin
Watts 1974)
Archaeology—Visual Books (Macdonald Educational)
The Pegasus Book of Archaeology by Geoffrey Palmer and
Noel Lloyd (Dennis Dobson)
Archaeology by Jim Ingram (Michael Joseph)
Darwin and the Beagle by Alan Moorehead (Hardback –
Hamish Hamilton, Paperback – Penguin Books)
Charles Darwin by Arthur S. Gregor (Angus and
Robertson)
The Life of Monkeys and Apes by Michael Boorer
(Macdonald Educational)
Apes and Monkeys by Desmond Morris (Bodley Head)
In the Shadow of Man by Jane Goodall (Collins)
The Kon-Tiki Expedition by Thor Heyerdahl (Allen &
Unwin)
The Ra Expeditions by Thor Heyerdahl (Allen & Unwin)
Aku-Aku by Thor Heyerdahl (Allen & Unwin)

The Challenge of the Elements

Amy Johnson by Constance Babington Smith (Collins)
Gipsy Moth Circles the World by Sir Francis Chichester
(Hodder and Stoughton)
Lone Adventurer : the story of Sir Francis Chichester
by John Rowland (Lutterworth)

The Ocean World of Jacques Cousteau (Angus and
Robertson)
The Silent World by Jacques Cousteau (Hamish
Hamilton)
Man of Everest, the autobiography of Tenzing told to
James Ramsey Ullman (Harrap)

Impressions of Adventure

Mark Twain and his World by Justin Kaplan (Michael
Joseph)
The Adventures of Tom Sawyer by Mark Twain
(Penguin)
The Adventures of Huckleberry Finn by Mark Twain
(Penguin)
Life on the Mississippi by Mark Twain (Penguin)
Roughing It by Mark Twain (Penguin)
Gauguin by Alan Bowness (Phaidon)
*Scott's Last Voyage : through the Antarctic camera of
Herbert Ponting*, edited by Ann Savours (Sidgwick and
Jackson)
Captain Scott by Rowland Purton (McGraw Hill)

More Pioneers

Marco Polo by Charles Graves (Muller)
Across the Top of the World by Wally Herbert (Longman)
100 Great Adventures edited by John Canning (Odhams)
Sea Adventures by Graeme Cook (Macdonald and
Jane's)
New World Explorers by Louise Dickinson Rich
(Franklin Watts)
Discoverers and Adventurers by R. J. Unstead (A. & C.
Black)
Discoverers of the New World by Josef Berger (Caravel/
Cassell)
The Discovery of America by J. R. L. Anderson (Longman
Young)
Life at the Poles by G. L. Duddington (McGraw-Hill)
Roald Amundsen by Cateau DeLeeuw (Muller)
Amerigo Vespucci by Faith Yingling Knoop (Muller)
Henry Morton Stanley by Charles P. Graves (Muller)

How Expeditions are Organized

Overland by Peter Fraenkel (David and Charles)
Expeditions the Experts' Way by John Blashford-Snell
and Alistair Ballantine

FILMS

Lawrence of Arabia, an epic film starring Peter O'Toole
Inn of the Sixth Happiness, the story of Gladys Aylward
with Ingrid Bergman playing the leading role
Scott of the Antarctic
The Adventures of Huckleberry Finn

Index

12 3 4 5 6 7 8 9 Csd 84 89 82 81 80 79